Finger Looping is an easy and fun way to knit without using knitting needles. Bernat® Alize® EZ-Blanket™ yarn makes this possible by featuring preformed loops. Now, anyone can make perfect, uniform stitches by simply pulling one loop through another. Made with an ultra-soft chenille, this yarn is perfect for blankets, pillows, cowls, or anything else you'd want to cozy up with.

TABLE OF **CONTENTS**

- 4 EZ Afghan
- 5 EZ Cowl
- 6 EZ Baby Blanket
- 7 EZ Scarf
- 8 EZ Checked Blanket
- 11 EZ Cable Cowl
- 12 EZ Baby Bear Hat
- 14 EZ Criss-Cross Afghan
- 15 EZ Garter Ridge Cowl
- 16 EZ Two-Color Criss-Cross Pillow
- 18 EZ Spaced Garter Ridge Blanket
- 19 EZ Criss-Cross Scarf
- 20 EZ Diamond Lattice Blanket
- 23 EZ Garter Scarf
- 24 EZ Textures Blanket
- 26 EZ Round Pillow
- 28 EZ Criss-Cross Cowl
- 30 EZ Criss-Cross Baby Blanket
- 32 EZ Garter Ridge Pillow

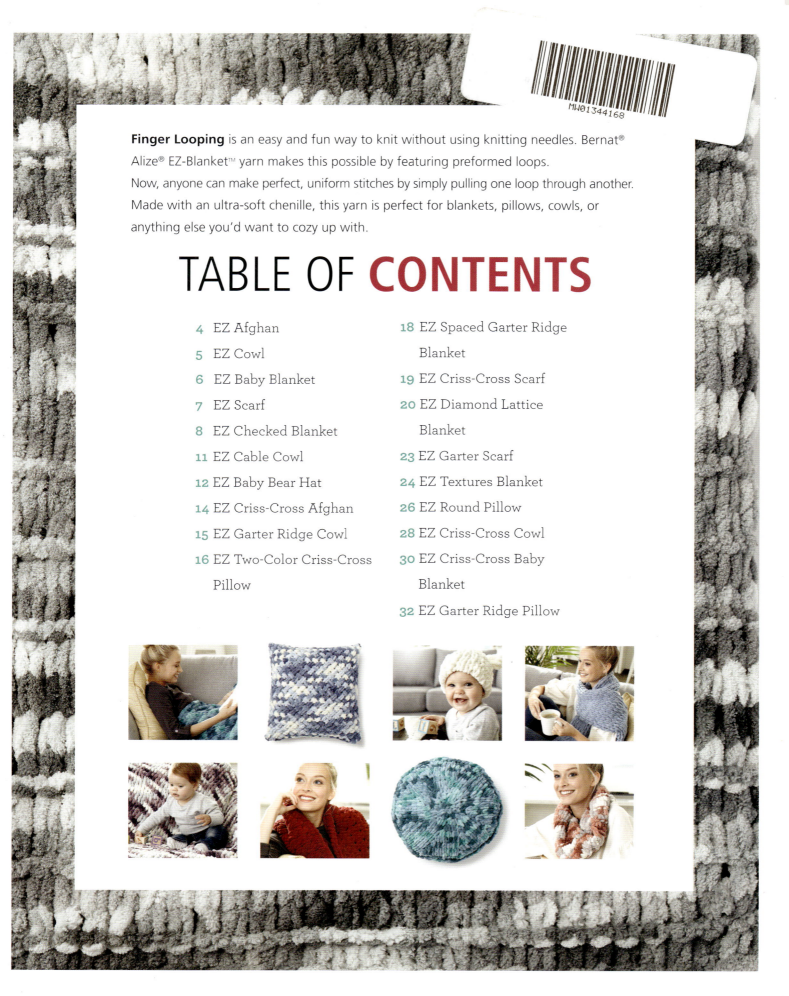

HOW TO
LEARN FINGER LOOPING

Creating a Foundation Row

The first step to begin any project is to create a foundation row. This foundation row is the number of loops needed to start a project, as specified in the pattern.

Starting at the end of the yarn, count out the necessary number of loops, also called stitches, and lay them out on a table. The pattern will say whether the end of the foundation row should be on the right or left. The rest of the yarn, called the working yarn, will be placed at the opposite side. Always arrange the loops of the foundation row so they point in the same direction away from you.

Begin Finger Looping

Rows can be worked from *left to right* or from *right to left*, but the basic action is the same: pull the next loop from the working yarn up through a stitch of the previous row.

For example, if there are 12 loops, also known as stitches, in the foundation row, pull the 13th stitch (next loop from the working yarn) up through the 12th stitch (last loop in the foundation row) *from behind*. Then pull the 14th stitch (next loop from the working yarn) up through the 11th stitch (next loop in the foundation row). Continue in this manner until you have reached the end of the row.

Each subsequent row is worked the same way, but in the opposite direction as the last row. You will not need to turn the work after you complete a row. The right side will be facing at all times. The photos below show an example of a row being worked from *left to right*.

Bind Off

When you reach the end of a project, you must bind off, meaning to close off the loops so they cannot be pulled out.

Working in the same direction as the last row worked, pull the 2nd loop through the 1st loop. Pull the 3rd loop through the 2nd loop. Continue in this manner to the end of row. One open loop will remain. Cut the last loop to create a yarn tail, and then tie to secure it in place.

VARIATIONS

Always carefully read the instructions. The instructions describe whether each row should be worked from *left to right* or *right to left*.

Many patterns require holding the working yarn behind the project and pulling the next loop up *from behind*. However, some patterns may require holding the working yarn in front of the project and pulling the next loop from the working yarn *towards the back*. Where you hold the yarn and whether you pull it *from behind* or *towards the back* affects the look of the project.

Other variations, like working in the round (EZ Baby Bear Hat) or color blocking (EZ Checked Blanket) are incorporated throughout. Each pattern clearly describes how to work the necessary variations.

Criss-Cross Patterns

Some patterns create cables or woven textures by crossing stitches in front of each other and working them in a new order. This may seem confusing at first, but carefully read the instructions for exactly how this should be worked.

When binding off criss-cross projects, do so in the same manner as before. Working in the same direction as the last row worked, pull the 2nd loop through the 1st loop. Pull the 3rd loop through the 2nd loop. Continue in this manner to the end of the row. One open loop will remain. Follow the instructions to complete the project. Cut the last loop to create a yarn tail, and then tie to secure it in place.

EZ AFGHAN

Beginner

MEASUREMENTS
Approx 51 x 60"/129.5 x 152.5cm

MATERIALS
Yarn
Bernat® Alize® Blanket-EZ™, 6.4oz/180g balls, each approx 18yd/16m (polyester)
- 6 balls in 37019 Seaport Teals

NOTES
1) When beginning project, yarn end can start at far right or far left. Instructions are written with yarn end starting on the far right. Please reverse direction throughout the pattern if the opposite is more comfortable.
2) Right side of project is facing at all times.
3) Working yarn is held behind stitches throughout work.
4) Loops from working yarn are always pulled through stitches from back to front of work.

AFGHAN
Count 65 loops for foundation row (noting yarn end is at far right and all loops are facing upwards).

1st row Working from *left to right*, pull the 66th loop (from working yarn) up through 65th loop (last loop of foundation row) from behind to create a knit stitch. Pull next loop from working yarn up through next loop of foundation. Continue in this manner to end of row. Do *not* turn work. 65 stitches in row.

2nd row Working from *right to left*, pull next loop from working yarn up from behind through last stitch worked on previous row. *Pull next loop from working yarn up from behind through next stitch. Repeat from * across to end of row. Do *not* turn.

3rd row Working from *left to right*, pull next loop from working yarn up from behind through last stitch worked on previous row. *Pull next loop from working yarn up from behind through next stitch. Repeat from * across to end of row. Do *not* turn.

Repeat 2nd and 3rd rows until Afghan measures approximately 60"/152.5cm, ending on a 3rd row.

Bind-off row Working in *same direction as last row*, pull 2nd stitch through first stitch. Pull 3rd stitch through 2nd stitch. Pull 4th stitch through 3rd stitch. Continue in this manner to end of row. Cut last loop to create a yarn tail. Tie to secure and weave in ends.●

LEARN BY VIDEO
Learn to use Bernat® Alize® Blanket-EZ™.
Watch the *"EZ Knitting: Stocking Stitch"* tutorial on YouTube.

EZ COWL

Beginner

MEASUREMENTS
Approx 16"/40.5cm deep x 24"/61cm around

MATERIALS
Yarn
Bernat® Alize® Blanket-EZ™, 6.4oz/180g balls, approx 18yd/16m (polyester)
• 1 ball in 37013 Cream

NOTES
1) When beginning project, yarn end can start at far right or far left. Instructions are written with yarn end starting on the far right. Please reverse direction throughout the pattern if the opposite is more comfortable.
2) Right side of project is always facing (until seaming).
3) Working yarn is held behind stitches throughout work.
4) Loops from working yarn are always pulled through stitches from back to front of work.

COWL
Count 20 loops for foundation row (noting yarn end is at far right and all loops are facing upwards).
1st row Working from *left to right*, pull the 21st loop (from working yarn) up through 20th loop (last loop of foundation row) from behind to create a knit stitch. Pull next loop from working yarn up through next loop of foundation. Continue in this manner to end of row. Do *not* turn work. 20 stitches in row.
2nd row Working from *right to left*, pull next loop from working yarn up from behind through last stitch worked on previous row. *Pull next loop from working yarn up from behind through next stitch. Repeat from * across to end of row. Do *not* turn.
3rd row Working from *left to right*, pull next loop from working yarn up from behind through last stitch worked on previous row. *Pull next loop from working yarn up from behind through next stitch. Repeat from * across to end of row. Do *not* turn.
Repeat 2nd and 3rd rows until work measures approximately 24"/61cm, ending on a 3rd row.
Bind-off row Working in *same direction as last row*, pull 2nd stitch through first stitch. Pull 3rd stitch through 2nd stitch. Pull 4th stitch through 3rd stitch. Continue in this manner to end of row. Leave at least 15"/38cm of working yarn attached for seaming.

Seam
Fold Cowl in half (with right sides facing together). Working along top and bottom edges, pull first loop from working yarn up through both thicknesses. Working evenly along edge, pull 2nd loop up through both thicknesses. Pull first loop through 2nd loop. Continue in this manner along edge. Cut last loop to create yarn tail. Pull yarn tail through last loop.
Tie to secure and weave in ends. Turn Cowl so right side is facing.●

LEARN BY VIDEO
Learn to use Bernat® Alize® Blanket-EZ™.
Watch the *"EZ Knitting: Stocking Stitch"* tutorial on YouTube.

EZ BABY BLANKET

Beginner

MEASUREMENTS
Approx 39"/99cm square

MATERIALS
Yarn

Bernat® Alize® Blanket-EZ™, 6.4oz/180g balls, each approx 18yd/16m (polyester)
- 3 balls in 37021 Thistle

NOTES
1) When beginning project, yarn end can start at far right or far left. Instructions are written with yarn end starting on the far right. Please reverse direction throughout the pattern if the opposite is more comfortable.
2) Right side of project is facing at all times.
3) Working yarn is held behind stitches throughout work.
4) Loops from working yarn are always pulled through stitches from back to front of work.

BLANKET
Count 50 loops for foundation row (noting yarn end is at far right and all loops are facing upwards).

1st row Working from *left to right*, pull the 51st loop (from working yarn) up through 50th loop (last loop of foundation row) from behind to create a knit stitch. Pull next loop from working yarn up through next loop of foundation row. Continue in this manner to end of row. Do *not* turn work. 50 stitches in row.

2nd row Working from *right to left*, pull next loop from working yarn up from behind through last stitch worked on previous row. *Pull next loop from working yarn up from behind through next stitch. Repeat from * across to end of row. Do *not* turn.

3rd row Working from *left to right*, pull next loop from working yarn up from behind through last stitch worked on previous row. *Pull next loop from working yarn up from behind through next stitch. Repeat from * across to end of row. Do *not* turn.

Repeat 2nd and 3rd rows until Blanket measures approximately 39"/99cm, ending on a 3rd row.

Bind-off row Working in *same direction as last row*, pull 2nd stitch through first stitch. Pull 3rd stitch through 2nd stitch. Pull 4th stitch through 3rd stitch. Continue in this manner to end of row. Cut last loop to create a yarn tail. Tie to secure and weave in ends.●

LEARN BY VIDEO
Learn to use Bernat® Alize® Blanket-EZ™.
Watch the *"EZ Knitting: Stocking Stitch"* tutorial on YouTube.

EZ SCARF

Beginner

MEASUREMENTS
Approx 10 x 74"/25.5 x 188cm

MATERIALS
Yarn
Bernat® Alize® Blanket-EZ™, 6.4oz/180g balls, each approx 18yd/16m (polyester)
• 2 balls in 37018 Country Blue

NOTES
1) When beginning project, yarn end can start at far right or far left. Instructions are written with yarn end starting on the far right. Please reverse direction throughout the pattern if the opposite is more comfortable.
2) Right side of project is facing at all times.
3) Working yarn is held behind stitches throughout work.
4) Loops from working yarn are always pulled through stitches from back to front of work.

SCARF
Count 12 loops for foundation row (noting yarn end is at far right and all loops are facing upwards).

1st row Working from *left to right*, pull the 13th loop (from working yarn) up through 12th loop (last loop of foundation row) from behind to create a knit stitch. Pull next loop from working yarn up through next loop of foundation. Continue in this manner to end of row. Do *not* turn. 12 stitches in row.

2nd row Working from *right to left*, pull next loop from working yarn up from behind through last stitch worked on previous row. *Pull next loop from working yarn up from behind through next stitch. Repeat from * across to end of row. Do *not* turn.

3rd row Working from *left to right*, pull next loop from working yarn up from behind through last stitch worked on previous row. *Pull next loop from working yarn up from behind through next stitch. Repeat from * across to end of row. Do *not* turn.

Repeat 2nd and 3rd rows until Scarf measures approximately 74"/188cm, ending on a 2nd row.

Bind-off row Working in *same direction as last row*, pull 2nd stitch through first stitch. Pull 3rd stitch through 2nd stitch. Pull 4th stitch through 3rd stitch. Continue in this manner to end of row. Cut last loop to create a yarn tail. Tie to secure and weave in ends.•

LEARN BY VIDEO
Learn to use Bernat® Alize® Blanket-EZ™.
Watch the *"EZ Knitting: Stocking Stitch"* tutorial on YouTube.

EZ CHECKED BLANKET

Experienced

MEASUREMENTS
Approx 52"/132cm square

MATERIALS
Yarn

Bernat® Alize® Blanket-EZ™, 6.4oz/180g balls, each approx 18yd/16m (polyester)
- 2 balls in 37013 Cream (MC)
- 3 balls in 37014 Dark Gray (A)
- 2 balls in 37015 Black (B)

Notions
- 6 large stitch holders

NOTES
1) Right side of work is facing at all times.
2) Working yarn is held behind stitches throughout.
3) Loops from working yarn are always pulled through stitches from back to front of work.

MC	A	MC	A	MC	A	MC
A	B	A	B	A	B	A
MC	A	MC	A	MC	A	MC
A	B	A	B	A	B	A
MC	A	MC	A	MC	A	MC
A	B	A	B	A	B	A
MC	A	MC	A	MC	A	MC
Strip Seven	Strip Six	Strip Five	Strip Four	Strip Three	Strip Two	Strip One

BLANKET
Strip One

With MC, count 11 loops for foundation row, noting yarn end is at far right and all loops are facing upwards.

1st row Working from *left to right*, pull the 12th loop (from working yarn) up through 11th loop (last loop of foundation row) from behind to create a knit stitch. Pull next loop from working yarn up through next loop of foundation. Continue in this manner to end of row. Do *not* turn work. 11 stitches in row.

2nd row Working from *right to left*, pull next loop from working yarn up from behind through last stitch worked on previous row.*Pull next loop from working yarn up from behind through next stitch. Repeat from * across to end of row. Do *not* turn.

3rd row Working from *left to right*, pull next loop from working yarn up from behind through last stitch worked on previous row. *Pull next loop from working yarn up from behind through next stitch. Repeat from * across to end of row. Do *not* turn.

4th row As 2nd row.

Repeat 3rd and 4th rows twice more, for a total of 8 rows worked. Cut thread at base of next loop (thread used to create the loop) to create a yarn tail. You will now join A. Cut thread at base of first loop of A to create a yarn tail. Tie tails of MC and A together, and weave in ends.

Continue with A, working as given for first 8 rows. Continue in this manner, working 8 rows with MC and 8 rows with A, until a total of 56 rows have been worked. Do *not* bind off. Leave stitches on stitch holder to secure.

LEARN BY VIDEO
Learn to use Bernat® Alize® Blanket-EZ™.
Watch the *"EZ Knitting: Checkered Blanket"* tutorial on YouTube.

Strip Two

With A, count 11 loops for foundation row, noting yarn end is at far right and all loops are facing upwards.

1st row Working from *left to right*, pull the 12th loop (from working yarn) up through 11th loop (last loop of foundation row) from behind to create a knit stitch. Pull next loop from working yarn up through next loop of foundation. Continue in this manner to last loop of foundation row. Place last loop of foundation row over far left loop of first row of Strip One; pull next loop from working yarn up through *both* loops. Do *not* turn work. 11 stitches in row.

2nd row Working from *right to left*, pull next loop from working yarn up from behind through first loop of second row of Strip One *and* last stitch worked on previous row. *Pull next loop from working yarn up from behind through next stitch. Repeat from * across to end of row. Do *not* turn.

3rd row Working from *left to right*, pull next loop from working yarn up from behind through last stitch

EZ CHECKED BLANKET

worked on previous row. *Pull next loop from working yarn up from behind through next stitch. Repeat from * to last loop. Pull next loop of working yarn up from behind through first loop of third row of Strip One and last loop of previous row. Do *not* turn. Continue in this manner, joining work in an ascending manner up left edge of Strip One, until 8 rows have been worked. Cut thread at base of next loop (thread used to create the loop) to create a yarn tail. You will now join B. Cut thread at base of first loop of B to create a yarn tail. Tie tails of A and B together, and weave in ends. Continue with B, working as given for first 8 rows. Continue in this manner, working 8 rows with A and 8 rows with B, until a total of 56 rows have been worked. Do *not* bind off. Leave stitches on stitch holder to secure.

Strips Three to Six
Following the color layout shown in Diagram, continue working as established for Strips Three to Six, joining sides of Strips as before and leaving stitches for each Strip on stitch holder to secure.

Strip Seven
With MC, count 10 loops for foundation row, noting yarn end is at far right and all loops are facing upwards.
1st row Working from *left to right*, pull the 11th loop (from working yarn) up through 10th loop (last loop of foundation row) from behind to create a knit stitch. Pull next loop from working yarn up through next loop of foundation. Continue in this manner to last loop of foundation row. Place last loop of foundation row over far left loop of first row of Strip Six; pull next loop from working yarn up through *both* loops. Do *not* turn work. 10 stitches in row.
2nd row Working from *right to left*, pull next loop from working yarn up from behind through first loop of second row of Strip Six *and* last stitch worked on previous row. *Pull next loop from working yarn up from behind through next stitch. Repeat from * across to end of row. Do *not* turn.
3rd row Working from *left to right*, pull next loop from working yarn up from behind through last stitch worked on previous row. *Pull next loop from working yarn up from behind through next stitch. Repeat from * to last loop. Pull next loop of working yarn up from behind through first loop of third row of Strip Six and last loop of previous row. Do *not* turn.
Continue in this manner, joining work in an ascending manner up left edge of Strip Six, until 8 rows have been worked.

Cut thread at base of next loop (thread used to create the loop) to create a yarn tail. You will now join A. Cut thread at base of first loop of MC to create a yarn tail. Tie tails of MC and A together, and weave in ends. Continue with A, working as given for first 8 rows. Continue in this manner, working 8 rows with MC and 8 rows with A, until a total of 56 rows have been worked. Do *not* bind off.

Bind-off row Working in *same direction as last row*, across all stitches from stitch holders from all Strips, pull 2nd stitch through first stitch. Pull 3rd stitch through 2nd stitch. Pull 4th stitch through 3rd stitch. Continue in this manner to end of row. Cut last loop to create yarn tail. Tie to secure and weave in ends.•

EZ CABLE COWL

Easy

MEASUREMENTS
Approx 11"/28cm deep x 44"/112cm around

MATERIALS
Yarn
Bernat® Alize® Blanket-EZ™, 6.4oz/180g balls, each approx 18yd/16m (polyester)
• 2 balls in 37017 Burgundy

NOTES
1) Right side of work is facing at all times (until seaming).
2) Working yarn is held behind stitches throughout.
3) Loops from working yarn are always pulled through stitches from back to front of work.

COWL
Count 64 loops for foundation row, noting yarn end is at far right and all loops are facing upwards.

1st row Working from *left to right*, pull 65th loop (from working yarn) up through 64th loop (last loop of foundation row) from behind to create a knit stitch. Pull next loop from working yarn up through next loop of foundation row. Continue in this manner to end of row. Do *not* turn work. 64 stitches in row.

2nd row Working from *right to left*, pull next loop from working yarn up from behind through last stitch worked on previous row. *Cross next stitch in front of 2nd stitch. Pull next loop from working yarn up from behind first crossed stitch. Pull next loop from working yarn up from behind 2nd crossed stitch. Rep from * to last stitch. Pull next loop from working yarn up from behind through last stitch. Do *not* turn.

3rd row Working from *left to right*, pull next loop from working yarn up from behind through last stitch worked on previous row. *Pull next loop from working yarn up from behind through next stitch. Repeat from * across to end of row. Do *not* turn.

Repeat 2nd and 3rd rows 6 times more.

Bind-off row Working in *same direction as last row*, pull 2nd stitch through first stitch. Pull 3rd stitch through 2nd stitch. Pull 4th stitch through 3rd stitch. Continue in this manner to end of row. Leave at least 15"/38cm of working yarn attached for seaming.

Seam
Fold Cowl in half lengthwise, with right sides facing together. Pass next loop of working yarn through both layers of Cowl, working between first and 2nd stitch of each edge. Continue passing loops through both layers until you have reached the opposite edge. Working from top to bottom, pull 2nd stitch through first stitch. Pull 3rd stitch through 2nd stitch. Pull 4th stitch through 3rd stitch. Continue in this manner to end of seam. Cut last loop to create a yarn tail. Tie to secure and weave in ends. Turn Cowl so right side is facing. •

LEARN BY VIDEO
Learn to use Bernat® Alize® Blanket-EZ™.
Watch the *"EZ Knitting: Cable Cowl"* tutorial on YouTube.

EZ BABY BEAR HAT

Intermediate

SIZE
One size to fit baby 1–2 yrs.

MATERIALS
Yarn
Bernat® Alize® Blanket-EZ™, 6.4oz/180g ball, approx 18yd/16m (polyester)
• 1 ball in 37013 Cream

Notions
• Removable stitch marker
• Sewing thread and needle

NOTES
1) Right side of work is facing at all times.
2) Working yarn is held behind stitches throughout.
3) Loops from working yarn are always pulled through stitches from back to front of work.
4) Move stitch marker at end of each round to mark end of round.

HAT
Cut first loop of yarn close to base to create a tail approximately 3"/7.5cm long. Count 24 loops for foundation round. Tie tail to yarn between 24th and 25th loops to create ring. Place all loops facing upwards.

1st rnd Working from *right to left*, pull first loop from working yarn up through first loop of round (first loop to the left of tie) to create a knit stitch. Pull next loop from working yarn up through next loop of foundation round. Continue in this manner to end of round. Place stitch marker between first and last stitches of round to mark end of round.

2nd rnd Working from *right to left*, pull first loop from working yarn up through first stitch of round. Pull next loop from working yarn up through next stitch of round. Continue in this manner to end of round. Repeat last round 6 times more (8 rounds worked in total).

Shape Top
1st rnd *Place first loop of round on top of second loop creating double loop (treat this double loop as 1 stitch). Pull next loop from working yarn up through double stitch (decrease made). Work next 2 stitches as usual. Repeat from * around—6 stitches decreased, 18 stitches remain.

2nd rnd *Make decrease. Work next stitch as usual. Repeat from * around—6 stitches decreased, 12 stitches remain.

LEARN BY VIDEO
Learn to use Bernat® Alize® Blanket-EZ™.
Watch the *"EZ Knitting: Baby Bear Hat"* tutorial on YouTube.

3rd rnd *Make decrease. Repeat from * around—6 stitches decreased, 6 stitches remain.

Close Top

Cut between next 2 loops of working yarn. Cut next loop from working yarn to create tail approximately 3"/7.5cm. Pull tail through remaining 6 stitches and pull to close top, bringing tail to inside of Hat. Tie to any stitch at inside of Hat.

Ears (make 2)

Cut first loop of yarn close to base to create a tail approximately 3"/7.5cm long. Count 6 loops for foundation round. Tie tail to yarn after 6th loop to create ring. Place all loops facing upwards.

1st and 2nd rnds Work as given for Hat.

3rd rnd *Make decrease. Repeat from * around—3 stitches remain.

Cut yarn, closing top as given for Hat.

Using sewing thread, sew Ears to Hat as seen in picture.•

EZ CRISS-CROSS AFGHAN

Easy

MEASUREMENTS
Approx 41 x 54"/104 x 137cm

Materials
Yarn

Bernat® Alize® Blanket-EZ™, 6.4oz/180g balls, each approx 18yd/16m (polyester)
• 7 balls in 37016 Mauve

NOTES
1) Right side of work is facing at all times.
2) Working yarn is held behind stitches throughout.
3) Loops from working yarn are always pulled through stitches from back to front of work.

AFGHAN
Count 64 loops for foundation row, noting yarn end is at far left and all loops are facing upwards.

1st row Working from *right to left*, cross 64th loop in front of 63rd loop. Pull next loop from working yarn up from behind through 63rd loop. Pull next loop from working yarn up from behind 64th loop. *Cross next loop of foundation row in front of 2nd loop of foundation row. Holding crossed loops in position, pull next loop from working yarn up from behind through next loop. Pull next loop from working yarn up from behind through next loop. Repeat from * to end of row. Do *not* turn work. 64 stitches in row.

2nd row Working from *left to right*, skip first stitch of row just worked. Cross 2nd stitch in front of 3rd stitch. Holding crossed stitches in position, pull loop from working yarn up from behind through 3rd stitch. Pull next loop from working yarn up from behind 2nd stitch. *Cross next 2 stitches. Holding crossed stitches in position, pull next loop from working yarn up from behind through next stitch. Pull next loop from working yarn up from behind through next stitch. Repeat from * to last stitch. Leave last stitch unworked. Do *not* turn work.

3rd row Working from *right to left*, cross unworked stitch in front of 2nd stitch. Holding crossed stitches in position, pull next loop from working yarn up from behind through 2nd stitch. Pull next loop from working yarn up from behind through first stitch. *Cross next 2 stitches. Holding crossed stitches in position, pull next loop from working yarn up from behind through next stitch. Pull next loop from working yarn up from behind through next stitch. Repeat from * to end of row. Do *not* turn work.

Repeat 2nd and 3rd rows until Afghan measures approximately 54"/137cm, ending on a 2nd row.

Bind-off row Working in *same direction as last row*, pull 2nd stitch through first stitch. Pull 3rd stitch through 2nd stitch. Pull 4th stitch through 3rd stitch. Continue in this manner to end of row. Cut thread at base of loop (thread used to create the loop) to create a yarn tail. Tie to secure and weave in ends.•

LEARN BY VIDEO
Learn to use Bernat® Alize® Blanket-EZ™.
Watch the "EZ Knitting: The Criss Cross Stitch" tutorial on YouTube.

EZ GARTER RIDGE COWL

Easy

MEASUREMENTS
Approx 16"/40.5cm] deep x 24"/61cm around

MATERIALS
Yarn
Bernat® Alize® Blanket-EZ™, 6.4oz/180g balls, each approx 18yd/16m (polyester)
• 2 balls in 37022 Warm Clay

NOTES
1) When beginning project, yarn end can start at far right or far left. Instructions are written with yarn end starting on the far right. Please reverse direction throughout the pattern if the opposite is more comfortable.
2) Right side of project is always facing (until seaming).

COWL
Count 20 loops for foundation row (noting yarn end is at far right and all loops are facing upwards).

1st row Working from *left to right*, pull the 21st loop (from working yarn) up through 20th loop (last loop of foundation row) from behind to create a knit stitch. Pull next loop from working yarn up through next loop of foundation row. Continue in this manner to end of row. Do *not* turn work. 20 stitches in row.

2nd row Working from *right to left*, with working yarn in *front*, pull next loop from working yarn *towards back* through last stitch worked on previous row. *Pull next loop from working yarn *towards back* through next stitch. Repeat from * across to end of row. Do *not* turn.

3rd row Working from *left to right*, with working yarn in *back*, pull next loop from working yarn up *from behind* through last stitch worked on previous row. *Pull next loop from working yarn up *from behind* through next stitch. Repeat from * across to end of row. Do *not* turn.

Repeat 2nd and 3rd rows until Cowl measures approximately 24"/61cm, ending on a 3rd row.

Bind-off row Working in *same direction as last row*, pull 2nd stitch through first stitch. Pull 3rd stitch through 2nd stitch. Pull 4th stitch through 3rd stitch. Continue in this manner to end of row. Leave at least 15"/38cm of working yarn attached for seaming.

Seam
Fold Cowl in half (with right sides facing together). Working along top and bottom edges, pull first loop from working yarn up through both thicknesses. Working evenly along edge, pull 2nd loop up through both thicknesses. Pull first loop through 2nd loop. Continue in this manner along edge. Cut last loop to create yarn tail. Pull yarn tail through last loop. Tie to secure and weave in ends. Turn Cowl so right side is facing.•

LEARN BY VIDEO
Learn to use Bernat® Alize® Blanket-EZ™.
Watch the *"EZ Knitting: The Garter Stitch"* tutorial on YouTube.

EZ TWO-COLOR CRISS-CROSS PILLOW

Easy

MEASUREMENTS
Approx 20"/51cm square

MATERIALS
Yarn
Bernat® Alize® Blanket-EZ™, 6.4oz/180g balls, each approx 18yd/16m (polyester)
- 2 balls in 37015 Black (A)
- 2 balls in 37013 Cream (B)

Notions
- 20"/51cm square pillow form
- Tapestry needle

NOTES
1) Right side of work is facing at all times.
2) Working yarn is held behind stitches throughout.
3) Loops from working yarn are always pulled through stitches from back to front of work.
4) Carry yarn when not in use up side of work.

PILLOW
With A, count 30 loops for foundation row, noting yarn end is at far left and all loops are facing upwards.
1st row Working from *right to left*, cross 30th loop in front of 29th loop. Pull next loop from working yarn up from behind through 29th loop. Pull next loop from working yarn up from behind 30th loop. *Cross next loop of foundation row in front of 2nd loop of foundation row. Holding crossed loops in position, pull next loop from working yarn up from behind through next loop. Pull next loop from working yarn up from behind through next loop. Repeat from * to end of row. Do *not* turn work. 30 stitches in row.
2nd row Working from *left to right*, skip first stitch of row just worked. Cross 2nd stitch in front of 3rd stitch. Holding crossed stitches in position, pull loop from working yarn up from behind through 3rd stitch. Pull next loop from working yarn up from behind 2nd stitch. *Cross next 2 stitches. Holding crossed stitches in position, pull next loop from working yarn up from behind through next stitch. Pull next loop from working yarn up from behind through next stitch. Repeat from * to last stitch. Leave last stitch unworked. Do *not* turn work.
3rd row Join B and working from *right to left*, cross unworked stitch in front of 2nd stitch. Holding crossed stitches in position, pull next loop from working yarn (B) up from behind through 2nd stitch. Pull next loop from working yarn up from behind through first stitch. *Cross next 2 stitches. Holding crossed stitches in position, pull next loop from working yarn up from behind through next stitch. Pull next loop from working yarn up from behind through next stitch. Repeat from * to end of row. Do *not* turn work.
4th row With B, as 2nd row.
5th row Join A, as 3rd row.
6th row With A, as 2nd row.
Repeat 3rd to 6th rows until Pillow measures approximately 40"/101.5cm, ending on a 4th or 6th row.
Bind-off row With same color yarn as last row worked, working in *same direction as last row*, pull 2nd stitch through first stitch. Pull 3rd stitch through 2nd stitch. Pull 4th stitch through 3rd stitch. Continue in this manner to end of row. Cut thread at base of loop (thread used to create the loop) to create a yarn tail.

LEARN BY VIDEO
Learn to use Bernat® Alize® Blanket-EZ™.
Watch the "*EZ Knitting: Two Color Criss-Cross Pillow*" tutorial on YouTube.

Tie to secure and weave in ends.

FINISHING

Fold work in half with right side facing out. Cut a length of yarn approximately 40"/101.5cm long. Cut thread at base of all loops to create a smooth yarn for seaming. Thread yarn onto tapestry needle. Sew 2 sides of Pillow closed. Insert pillow form. Sew remaining side closed.•

EZ SPACED GARTER RIDGE
BLANKET

Easy

MEASUREMENTS
Approx 50 x 56"/127 x 142cm

MATERIALS
Yarn

Bernat® Alize® Blanket-EZ™, 6.4oz/180g balls, each approx 18yd/16m (polyester)
- 5 balls in 37024 Slate Grays

NOTES
1) When beginning project, yarn end can start at far right or far left. Instructions are written with yarn end starting on the far right. Please reverse direction throughout the pattern if the opposite is more comfortable.

2) Right side of project is facing at all times.

BLANKET
Count 62 loops for foundation row (noting yarn end is at far right and all loops are facing upwards).

1st row Working from *left to right*, pull the 63rd loop (from working yarn) up through 62nd loop (last loop of foundation row) *from behind* to create a knit stitch. Pull next loop from working yarn up through next loop of foundation row. Continue in this manner to end of row. Do *not* turn work. 62 stitches in row.

2nd row Working from *right to left*, with working yarn in *front*, pull next loop from working yarn *towards back* through last stitch worked on previous row. *Pull next loop from working yarn *towards back* through next stitch. Repeat from * across to end of row. Do *not* turn.

3rd row Working from *left to right*, with working yarn in *back*, pull next loop from working yarn up *from behind* through last stitch worked on previous row. *Pull next loop from working yarn up *from behind* through next stitch. Repeat from * across to end of row. Do *not* turn.

4th and 5th rows Work as 2nd and 3rd rows.

6th row Working from *right to left*, with working yarn in *back*, pull next loop from working yarn up *from behind* through last stitch worked on previous row. *Pull next loop from working yarn up *from behind* through next stitch. Repeat from * across to end of row. Do *not* turn.

7th row Work as 3rd row.

8th row Work as 6th row.

9th row Work as 3rd row.

Repeat 2nd to 9th rows until Blanket measures approximately 51"/129.5cm, ending on a 9th row. Repeat 2nd to 5th rows once more.

Bind-off row Working in *same direction as last row*, pull 2nd stitch through first stitch. Pull 3rd stitch through 2nd stitch. Pull 4th stitch through 3rd stitch. Continue in this manner to end of row. Cut last loop to create yarn tail. Tie to secure and weave in ends.•

LEARN BY VIDEO
Learn to use Bernat® Alize® Blanket-EZ™.
Watch the *"EZ Knitting: Spaced Garter Ridge Blanket"* tutorial on YouTube.

EZ CRISS-CROSS SCARF

Easy

MEASUREMENTS
Approx 9 x 74"/23 x 188cm

MATERIALS
Yarn
Bernat® Alize® Blanket-EZ™, 6.4oz/180g balls, each approx 18yd/16m (polyester)
• 2 balls in 37020 Denim Blues

NOTES
1) Right side of work is facing at all times.
2) Working yarn is held behind stitches throughout.
3) Loops from working yarn are always pulled through stitches from back to front of work.

SCARF
Count 14 loops for foundation row, noting yarn end is at far left and all loops are facing upwards.

1st row Working from *right to left*, cross 14th loop in front of 13th loop. Pull next loop from working yarn up from behind through 13th loop. Pull next loop from working yarn up from behind 14th loop. *Cross next loop of foundation row in front of 2nd loop of foundation row. Holding crossed loops in position, pull next loop from working yarn up from behind through next loop. Pull next loop from working yarn up from behind through next loop. Repeat from * to end of row. Do *not* turn work. 14 stitches in row.

2nd row Working from *left to right*, skip first stitch of row just worked. Cross 2nd stitch in front of 3rd stitch. Holding crossed stitches in position, pull loop from working yarn up from behind through 3rd stitch. Pull next loop from working yarn up from behind 2nd stitch. *Cross next 2 stitches. Holding crossed stitches in position, pull next loop from working yarn up from behind through next stitch. Pull next loop from working yarn up from behind through next stitch. Repeat from * to last stitch. Leave last stitch unworked. Do *not* turn work.

3rd row Working from *right to left*, cross unworked stitch in front of 2nd stitch. Holding crossed stitches in position, pull next loop from working yarn up from behind through 2nd stitch. Pull next loop from working yarn up from behind through first stitch. *Cross next 2 stitches. Holding crossed stitches in position, pull next loop from working yarn up from behind through next stitch. Pull next loop from working yarn up from behind through next stitch. Repeat from * to end of row. Do *not* turn work.

Repeat 2nd and 3rd rows until Scarf measures approximately 74"/188cm, ending on a 2nd row.

Bind-off row Working in *same direction as last row*, pull 2nd stitch through first stitch. Pull 3rd stitch through 2nd stitch. Pull 4th stitch through 3rd stitch. Continue in this manner to end of row. Cut thread at base of loop (thread used to create the loop) to create a yarn tail. Tie to secure and weave in ends.•

LEARN BY VIDEO
Learn to use Bernat® Alize® Blanket-EZ™.
Watch the *"EZ Knitting: The Criss Cross Stitch"* tutorial on YouTube.

EZ DIAMOND LATTICE BLANKET

Experienced

MEASUREMENTS
Approx 56"/142cm wide x 60"/152.5cm long

MATERIALS
Yarn

Bernat® Alize® Blanket-EZ™, 6.4oz/180g balls, each approx 18yd/16m (polyester)
- 7 balls in 37018 Country Blue

NOTES
1) Right side of project is facing at all times.
2) Working yarn is held behind stitches throughout work.

BLANKET
Count 68 loops for foundation row.

First row Working from *right to left*, pull the 69th loop (from working yarn) up through 68th loop (last loop of foundation row) from behind to create a knit stitch. Pull next loop from working yarn up through next loop of foundation row. *Cross second loop of foundation row in front of first loop of foundation row (to the right). Pull next loop from working yarn up from behind next loop. Pull next loop from working yarn up from behind next loop. Cross next loop of foundation row in front of 2nd loop of foundation row (to the left). Pull next loop from working yarn up from behind through next loop. Pull next loop from working yarn up from behind through next loop. (Pull next loop from working yarn up through next loop of foundation row) twice. Repeat from * to end of row. Do *not* turn work. 68 stitches in row.

2nd row Working from *left to right*, pull next loop from working yarn up from behind through last stitch worked on previous row. *Cross 2nd stitch over next stitch (to the left). Pull loop from working yarn up from behind through 2nd stitch. Pull next loop from working yarn up from behind first stitch. (Pull next loop from working yarn up from behind next loop) twice. Cross next stitch in front of 2nd stitch (to the right). Pull next loop from working yarn up from behind first stitch. Pull next loop from working yarn up from behind 2nd stitch. Rep from * to last stitch. Pull loop from working yarn up from behind next loop. Do *not* turn.

3rd row Working from *right to left*, cross 2nd stitch of previous row over first stitch (to the right). Pull loop from working yarn up from behind 2nd stitch. Pull next loop from working yarn up from behind first stitch. *(Pull next loop from working yarn up from behind next loop) over next 4 stitches. Cross 2nd stitch in front of next stitch (to the right). Pull next loop from working yarn up from behind 2nd stitch. Pull next loop from working yarn up from behind first stitch. Rep from * to last 6 stitches. *(Pull next loop from working yarn up from behind next loop) over next 4 stitches. Cross next stitch in front of 2nd stitch (to the left). Pull next loop from working yarn up from behind 2nd loop. Pull next loop from working yarn up from behind first loop. Do *not* turn.

4th row Working from *left to right*, pull next loop from working yarn up from behind through last stitch worked on previous row. *Cross next stitch in front of 2nd stitch (to the right). Pull next loop from working yarn up from behind 2nd loop. Pull next loop from working yarn up from behind first loop. (Pull next loop from working yarn up from behind next loop) twice. Cross 2nd stitch in front of next stitch (to the left). Pull next loop from working yarn up from behind 2nd loop, Pull next loop

LEARN BY VIDEO
Learn to use Bernat® Alize® Blanket-EZ™.
Watch the *"EZ Knitting: EZ Diamond Lattice Blanket"* tutorial on YouTube.

from working yarn up from behind first loop. Rep from * to last stitch. Pull next loop from working yarn up from behind next stitch. Do *not* turn.

5th row Working from *right to left*, (pull next loop from working yarn up from behind last stitch worked on previous row) twice. *Cross next stitch in front of 2nd stitch (to the left). Pull next loop from working yarn up from behind 2nd stitch. Pull next loop from working yarn up from behind first stitch. Cross 2nd stitch in front of next stitch (to the right). Pull next loop from working yarn up from behind 2nd stitch. Pull next loop from working yarn up from behind first stitch. (Pull next loop from working yarn up from behind next loop) twice. Rep from * to end of row. Do *not* turn.

6th row Working from *left to right*, (pull next loop from working yarn up from behind last stitch worked on previous row) three times. *Cross 2nd stitch in front of first stitch (to the left). Pull next loop from working yarn up from behind 2nd stitch. Pull next loop from working yarn up from behind first stitch. (Pull next loop

EZ DIAMOND LATTICE BLANKET

from working yarn up from behind next loop) over next 4 stitches. Rep from * to last 5 stitches. Cross 2nd stitch in front of first stitch (to the left). Pull next loop from working yarn up from behind 2nd stitch. Pull next loop from working yarn up from behind first stitch. (pull next loop from working yarn up from behind last stitch worked on previous row) three times. Do *not* turn.

7th row Working from *right to left*, (pull next loop from working yarn up from behind last stitch worked on previous row) twice. *Cross 2nd stitch in front of next stitch (to the right). Pull next loop from working yarn up from behind 2nd stitch. Pull next loop from working yarn up from behind first stitch. Cross next stitch in front of 2nd stitch (to the left). Pull next loop from working yarn up from behind 2nd stitch. Pull next loop from working yarn up from behind first stitch. (Pull next loop from working yarn up from behind next loop) twice. Rep from * to end of row. Do *not* turn.

8th row Working from *left to right*, pull next loop from working yarn up from behind through last stitch worked on previous row. *Cross 2nd stitch in front of next stitch (to the left). Pull next loop from working yarn up from behind 2nd stitch. Pull next loop from working yarn up from behind first stitch. (Pull next loop from working yarn up from behind next loop) twice. Cross next stitch in front of 2nd stitch (to the right). Pull next loop from working yarn up from behind 2nd loop. Pull next loop from working yarn up from behind first loop. Rep from * to last stitch. Pull next loop from working yarn up from behind next loop. Do *not* turn.

9th row Working from *right to left*, cross first stitch over 2nd stitch (to the left). Pull next loop from working yarn up from behind 2nd loop. *Pull next loop from working yarn up from behind first loop. (Pull next loop from working yarn up from behind next loop) over next 4 stitches. Cross 2nd stitch in front of next stitch (to the right). Pull next loop from working yarn up from behind 2nd stitch. Pull next loop from working yarn up from behind first stitch. Rep from * to last 6 stitches. (Pull next loop from working yarn up from behind next loop) over next 4 stitches. Cross 2nd stitch in front of next stitch (to the right). Pull next loop from working yarn up from behind 2nd stitch. Pull next loop from working yarn up from behind first stitch. Do *not* turn.

10th row Working from *left to right*, pull next loop from working yarn up from behind last stitch worked on previous row. Cross next stitch in front of 2nd stitch (to the left). Pull next loop from working yarn up from behind 2nd stitch. Pull next loop from working yarn up from behind first stitch. *(Pull next loop from working yarn up from behind next loop) twice. Cross 2nd stitch over next stitch (to the left). Pull next loop from working yarn up from behind 2nd stitch. Pull next loop from working yarn up from behind first stitch. Cross next stitch over 2nd stitch (to the right). Pull next loop from working yarn up from behind 2nd loop. Pull next loop from working yarn up from behind first loop. Rep from * to last 5 stitches. (Pull next loop from working yarn up from behind next loop) twice. Cross next stitch in front of 2nd stitch (to the left). Pull next loop from working yarn up from behind 2nd stitch. Pull next loop from working yarn up from behind first stitch. Pull next loop from working yarn up from behind last stitch. Do *not* turn.
Repeat 5th to 10th rows for pattern.
Work in pattern until Blanket measures approximately 60"/152.5cm, ending on a 5th row.

Bind-off row Working in *same direction as last row*, pull 2nd stitch through first stitch. Pull 3rd stitch through 2nd stitch. Pull 4th stitch through 3rd stitch. Continue in this manner to end of row. Cut thread at base of loop (thread used to create the loop) to create a yarn tail. Tie to secure and weave in end.•

EZ GARTER SCARF

Easy

MEASUREMENTS
Approx 9 x70"/23 x 178cm

MATERIALS
Yarn
Bernat® Alize® Blanket-EZ™, 6.4oz/180g balls, each approx 18yd/16m (polyester)
• 2 balls in 37016 Mauve

NOTES
1) When beginning project, yarn end can start at far right or far left. Instructions are written with yarn end starting on the far right. Please reverse direction throughout the pattern if the opposite is more comfortable.
2) Right side of project is facing at all times.

SCARF
Count 12 loops for foundation row (noting yarn end is at far right and all loops are facing upwards).

1st row Working from *left to right*, pull the 13th loop (from working yarn) up through 12th loop (last loop of foundation row) from behind to create a knit stitch. Pull next loop from working yarn up through next loop of foundation row. Continue in this manner to end of row. Do *not* turn. 12 stitches in row.

2nd row Working from *right to left* with working yarn in *front*, pull next loop from working yarn *towards back* through last stitch worked on previous row. *Pull next loop from working yarn *towards back* through next stitch. Repeat from * across to end of row. Do *not* turn.

3rd row Working from *left to right*, with working yarn in *back*, pull next loop from working yarn up *from behind* through last stitch worked on previous row. *Pull next loop from working yarn up *from behind* through next stitch. Repeat from * across to end of row. Do *not* turn.

Repeat 2nd and 3rd rows until Scarf measures approximately 70"/178cm, ending on a 2nd row.

Bind-off row Working in *same direction as last row*, pull 2nd stitch through first stitch. Pull 3rd stitch through 2nd stitch. Pull 4th stitch through 3rd stitch. Continue in this manner to end of row. Cut last loop to create yarn tail. Tie to secure and weave in ends.•

LEARN BY VIDEO
Learn to use Bernat® Alize® Blanket-EZ™.
Watch the *"EZ Knitting: The Garter Stitch"* tutorial on YouTube.

EZ TEXTURES BLANKET

Intermediate

MEASUREMENTS
Approx 56 x 60"/142 x 152.5cm

MATERIALS
Yarn

Bernat® Alize® Blanket-EZ™, 6.4oz/180g balls, each approx 18yd/16m (polyester)
- 8 balls in 37014 Dark Gray

NOTES
1) Right side of project is facing at all times.

BLANKET
Count 70 loops for foundation row (noting yarn end is far right and all loops are facing upwards).

1st row Working from *left to right*, twist the 70th loop (last loop of foundation row) once to the left. Pull the 71st loop (from working yarn) up through 70th loop from behind to create a twisted stitch. Twist next loop once to the left (of foundation row). Pull next loop from working yarn up through next loop of foundation row. Continue in this manner to end of row. Do *not* turn. 70 stitches in row.

2nd row Working from *right to left*, with working yarn in *front*, twist last stitch worked on previous row once to the left. Pull next loop from working yarn *towards back* through last stitch worked on previous row. *Twist next stitch once to left. Pull next loop from working yarn *towards back* through next stitch. Repeat from * across row to end of row. Do *not* turn.

3rd row Working from *left to right*, with working yarn in *back*, twist last stitch worked on previous row once to the left. Pull next loop from working yarn up *from behind* through last st worked on previous row. *Twist next stitch once to left. Pull next loop from working yarn up *from behind* through next stitch. Repeat from * across to end of row. Do *not* turn.

4th row As 2nd row.

Begin Cable Pattern

5th row Working from *left to right*, with working yarn in *back*, twist last stitch worked on previous row once to the left. Pull next loop from working yarn up *from behind* through last st worked on previous row. *Twist next stitch once to left. Pull next loop from working yarn up *from behind* through next stitch. Repeat from * 4 times more. (6 twisted stitches worked). **Cross next stitch in front of 2nd stitch. Pull next loop from working yarn up *from behind* first stitch. Pull next loop from working yarn up *from behind* 2nd stitch. Rep from ** to last 6 stitches. Twist next stitch once to left. Pull next loop from working yarn up *from behind* through next stitch over last 6 stitches. Do *not* turn.

6th row Working from *right to left*, with working yarn in *front*, twist last stitch worked on previous row once to the left. Pull next loop from working yarn *towards back* through last stitch worked on previous row. *Twist next stitch once to left. Pull next loop from working yarn *towards back* through next stitch. Repeat from * 4 times more (6 twisted stitches worked). Bring working yarn to *back*, **Pull next loop from working yarn up *from behind* through next stitch. Repeat from ** to last 6 sts. Bring working yarn to *front*, *twist next stitch once to left, Pull next loop from working yarn *towards back* through next stitch over last 6 stitches. Do *not* turn.

LEARN BY VIDEO
Learn to use Bernat® Alize® Blanket-EZ™.
Watch the "*EZ Knitting: Textures Blanket*" tutorial on YouTube.

Repeat last 2 rows for pattern until Blanket measures approximately 56"/142cm, ending on a 5th row.

Next row As 2nd row.

Next row As 3rd row.

Repeat last 2 rows once more.

Next row As 2nd row.

Bind-off row Working in *same direction as last row*, pull 2nd stitch through first stitch. Pull 3rd stitch through 2nd stitch. Pull 4th stitch through 3rd stitch. Continue in this manner to end of row. Cut last loop to create a yarn tail. Tie to secure and weave in end.•

EZ ROUND PILLOW

Intermediate

MEASUREMENTS
Approx 18"/45.5cm in diameter

MATERIALS
Yarn
Bernat® Alize® Blanket-EZ™, 6.4oz/180g balls, each approx 18yd/16m (polyester)
• 2 balls in 37019 Seaport Tealsa

Notions
• 18"/45.5cm round pillow form
• Removable stitch marker

NOTES
1) Right side of work is facing at all times.
2) Working yarn is held behind stitches throughout.
3) Loops from working yarn are always pulled through stitches from back to front of work.
4) To join a new ball of yarn, cut last loop of current ball of yarn close to its base to create a yarn tail. Cut first loop of new ball of yarn in the same manner. Tie 2 tails together.
5) Move stitch marker at end of each round to mark end of round.

PILLOW
Back
Cut first loop of yarn close to base to create a yarn tail. Count next 4 loops for foundation round. Tie tail to yarn between 4th and 5th loops to create ring. Place ring on a flat surface with loops pointing outward.
1st rnd Working counter-clockwise, pull first 2 loops from working yarn up through first loop of round (first loop to the left of tie) creating 2 knit stitches. *Pull next 2 loops from working yarn up through next loop of foundation round. Repeat from * twice more. Place stitch marker between first and last stitches of round to mark end of round—4 stitches increased, 8 stitches at end of round.
2nd rnd Pull first 2 loops from working yarn up through first stitch of round. *Pull next 2 loops from working yarn up through next stitch of round. Repeat from * 6 times more—8 stitches increased, 16 stitches at end of round.
3rd rnd Pull first 2 loops from working yarn up through first stitch. Pull next loop from working yarn up through next stitch. *Pull next 2 loops from working yarn up through next stitch. Pull next loop from working yarn up through next stitch. Repeat from * around—8 stitches increased, 24 stitches at end of round.

LEARN BY VIDEO
Learn to use Bernat® Alize® Blanket-EZ™.
Watch the "EZ Knitting: Round Pillow" tutorial on YouTube.

4th rnd Pull first 2 loops from working yarn up through first stitch. [Pull next loop from working yarn up through next stitch] twice. *Pull next 2 loops from working yarn up through next stitch. [Pull next loop from working yarn up through next stitch] twice. Repeat from * around—8 stitches increased, 32 stitches at end of round.

5th rnd Pull first 2 loops from working yarn up through first stitch. [Pull next loop from working yarn up through next stitch] 3 times. *Pull next 2 loops from working yarn up through next stitch. [Pull next loop from working yarn up through next stitch] 3 times. Repeat from * around—8 stitches increased, 40 stitches at end of round.

6th rnd Pull first 2 loops from working yarn up through first stitch. [Pull next loop from working yarn up through next stitch] 4 times. *Pull next 2 loops from working yarn up through next stitch. [Pull next loop from working yarn up through next stitch[4 times. Repeat from * around—8 stitches increased, 48 stitches at end of round.

7th rnd Pull first 2 loops from working yarn up through first stitch. [Pull next loop from working yarn up through next stitch] 5 times. *Pull next 2 loops from working yarn up through next stitch. [Pull next loop from working yarn up through next stitch] 5 times. Repeat from * around—8 stitches increased, 56 stitches at end of round.

8th rnd Pull first 2 loops from working yarn up through first stitch. [Pull next loop from working yarn up through next stitch] 6 times. *Pull next 2 loops from working yarn up through next stitch. [Pull next loop from working yarn up through next stitch] 6 times. Repeat from * around—8 stitches increased, 64 stitches at end of round.

9th rnd Pull first 2 loops from working yarn up through first stitch. [Pull next loop from working yarn up through next stitch] 7 times. *Pull next 2 loops from working yarn up through next stitch. [Pull next loop from working yarn up through next stitch] 7 times. Repeat from * around—8 stitches increased, 72 stitches at end of round.

10th rnd Pull first 2 loops from working yarn up through first stitch. [Pull next loop from working yarn up through next stitch] 8 times. *Pull next 2 loops from working yarn up through next stitch. [Pull next loop from working yarn up through next stitch] 8 times. Repeat from * around—8 stitches increased, 80 stitches at end of round.

Cut working yarn several loops away from last stitch.

FRONT

Make as given for Back but do *not* cut yarn at end of 10th round.

Join Front and Back

Place Front and Back together with edges aligned and wrong sides facing each other. Pull first loop of working yarn up through first stitch of Front and Back joining them together. *Pull next stitch of working yarn up through next stitch of Front and Back. Pull last stitch worked up through previous stitch worked (casting off one stitch). Repeat from * around, inserting pillow form half way through. One stitch remains.

Cut working yarn after next loop. Cut last loop of working yarn to create a yarn tail. Pull tail through remaining stitch. Tie tail to last stitch and tuck to inside of Pillow.•

EZ CRISS-CROSS COWL

Easy

MEASUREMENTS
Approx 16"/40.5cm deep x 26"/66cm around

MATERIALS
Yarn

Bernat® Alize® Blanket-EZ™, 6.4oz/180g ball, approx 18yd/16m (polyester)
- 1 ball in 37024 Slate Grays

NOTES
1) Right side of work is always facing (until seaming).
2) Working yarn is held behind stitches throughout.
3) Loops from working yarn are always pulled through stitches from back to front of work.

COWL
Count 20 loops for foundation row, noting yarn end is at far left and all loops are facing upwards.

1st row Working from *right to left*, cross 20th loop in front of 19th loop. Pull next loop from working yarn up from behind through 19th loop. Pull next loop from working yarn up from behind 20th loop. *Cross next loop of foundation row in front of 2nd loop of foundation row. Holding crossed loops in position, pull next loop from working yarn up from behind through next loop. Pull next loop from working yarn up from behind through next loop. Repeat from * to end of row. Do *not* turn work. 20 stitches in row.

2nd row Working from *left to right*, skip first stitch of row just worked. Cross 2nd stitch in front of 3rd stitch. Holding crossed stitches in position, pull loop from working yarn up from behind through 3rd stitch. Pull next loop from working yarn up from behind 2nd stitch. *Cross next 2 stitches. Holding crossed stitches in position, pull next loop from working yarn up from behind through next stitch. Pull next loop from working yarn up from behind through next stitch. Repeat from * to last stitch. Leave last stitch unworked. Do *not* turn work.

3rd row Working from *right to left*, cross unworked stitch in front of 2nd stitch. Holding crossed stitches in position, pull next loop from working yarn up from behind through 2nd stitch. Pull next loop from working yarn up from behind through first stitch. *Cross next 2 stitches. Holding crossed stitches in position, pull next loop from working yarn up from behind through next stitch. Pull next loop from working yarn up from behind through next stitch. Repeat from * to end of row. Do *not* turn work.

Repeat 2nd and 3rd rows until work measures

LEARN BY VIDEO
Learn to use Bernat® Alize® Blanket-EZ™.
Watch the *"EZ Knitting: Criss-Cross Cowl Tutorial"* on YouTube.

approximately 26"/66cm, ending on a 2nd row.
Bind-off row Working in *same direction as last row*, pull 2nd stitch through first stitch. Pull 3rd stitch through 2nd stitch. Pull 4th stitch through 3rd stitch. Continue in this manner to end of row. Leave at least 22 loops of working yarn attached for seaming.

Seam
Fold Cowl in half (with right sides facing together). Working along top and bottom edges, pull first loop from working yarn up through both thicknesses. Working evenly along edge, pull 2nd loop up through both thicknesses. Pull first loop through 2nd loop. Continue in this manner along edge. Cut last loop to create yarn tail. Pull yarn tail through last loop. Tie to secure and weave in ends. Turn cowl so right side is facing.•

EZ CRISS-CROSS BABY BLANKET

Easy

MEASUREMENTS
Approx 32 x 40"/81.5 x 101.5cm

MATERIALS
Yarn

Bernat® Alize® Blanket-EZ™, 6.4oz/180g balls, each approx 18yd/16m (polyester)
• 4 balls in 37013 Cream

NOTES
1) Right side of work is facing at all times.
2) Working yarn is held behind stitches throughout.
3) Loops from working yarn are always pulled through stitches from back to front of work.

BLANKET
Count 50 loops for foundation row, noting yarn end is at far left and all loops are facing upwards.

1st row Working from *right to left*, cross 50th loop in front of 49th loop. Pull next loop from working yarn up from behind through 49th loop. Pull next loop from working yarn up from behind 50th loop. *Cross next loop of foundation row in front of 2nd loop of foundation row. Holding crossed loops in position, pull next loop from working yarn up from behind through next loop. Pull next loop from working yarn up from behind through next loop. Repeat from * to end of row. Do *not* turn work. 50 stitches in row.

2nd row Working from *left to right*, skip first stitch of row just worked. Cross 2nd stitch in front of 3rd stitch. Holding crossed stitches in position, pull loop from working yarn up from behind through 3rd stitch. Pull next loop from working yarn up from behind 2nd stitch. *Cross next 2 stitches. Holding crossed stitches in position, pull next loop from working yarn up from behind through next stitch. Pull next loop from working yarn up from behind through next stitch. Repeat from * to last stitch. Leave last stitch unworked. Do *not* turn work.

3rd row Working from *right to left*, cross unworked stitch in front of 2nd stitch. Holding crossed stitches in position, pull next loop from working yarn up from behind through 2nd stitch. Pull next loop from working yarn up from behind through first stitch. *Cross next 2 stitches. Holding crossed stitches in position, pull next loop from working yarn up from behind through next stitch. Pull next loop from working yarn up from behind through next stitch. Repeat from * to end of row. Do *not* turn work.

Repeat 2nd and 3rd rows until Blanket measures

LEARN BY VIDEO
Learn to use Bernat® Alize® Blanket-EZ™.
Watch the *"EZ Knitting: The Criss Cross Stitch"* tutorial on YouTube.

approximately 40"/101.5cm, ending on a 2nd row.
Bind-off row Working in *same direction as last row*, pull 2nd stitch through first stitch. Pull 3rd stitch through 2nd stitch. Pull 4th stitch through 3rd stitch. Continue in this manner to end of row. Cut thread at base of loop (thread used to create the loop) to create a yarn tail. Tie to secure and weave in ends.•

EZ GARTER RIDGE PILLOW

Easy

MEASUREMENTS
Approx 20"/51cm square

MATERIALS
Yarn
Bernat® Alize® Blanket-EZ™, 6.4oz/180g balls, each approx 18yd/16m (polyester)
• 2 balls in 37021 Thistle

Notions
• 20"/51cm square pillow form
• Tapestry needle

NOTES
1) When beginning project, yarn end can start at far right or far left. Instructions are written with yarn end starting on the far right. Please reverse direction throughout the pattern if the opposite is more comfortable.
2) Right side of project is facing at all times.

PILLOW
Count 25 loops for foundation row (noting yarn end is at far right and all loops are facing upwards).

1st row Working from *left to right*, pull the 26th loop (from working yarn) up through 25th loop (last loop of foundation row) from behind to create a knit stitch. Pull next loop from working yarn up through next loop of foundation row. Continue in this manner to end of row. Do *not* turn. 25 stitches in row.

2nd row Working from *right to left*, with working yarn *in front*, pull next loop from working yarn *towards back* through last stitch worked on previous row. *Pull next loop from working yarn *towards back* through next stitch. Repeat from * across to end of row. Do *not* turn.

3rd row Working from *left to right*, with working yarn *in back*, pull next loop from working yarn up *from behind* through last stitch worked on previous row. *Pull next loop from working yarn up from behind through next stitch. Repeat from * across to end of row. Do *not* turn.

Repeat 2nd and 3rd rows until Pillow measures approximately 40"/101.5cm, ending on a 3rd row.

Bind-off row Working in *same direction as last row*, pull 2nd stitch through first stitch. Pull 3rd stitch through 2nd stitch. Pull 4th stitch through 3rd stitch. Continue in this manner to end of row. Cut last loop to create yarn tail. Tie to secure and weave in ends.

FINISHING
Fold work in half with right side facing out. Cut a length of yarn approx 40"/101.5cm long. Cut thread at base of all loops to create a smooth yarn for seaming. Thread yarn onto tapestry needle. Sew 2 sides of Pillow closed. Insert pillow form. Sew remaining side closed.•

LEARN BY VIDEO
Learn to use Bernat® Alize® Blanket-EZ™.
Watch the *"EZ Knitting: The Garter Stitch"* tutorial on YouTube.